The Toys

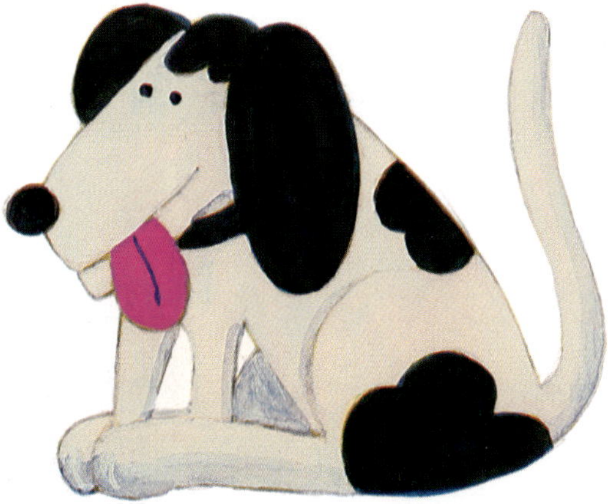

by Sarah Holliday
illustrated by Max Grover

Harcourt
Orlando Boston Dallas Chicago San Diego
www.harcourtschool.com

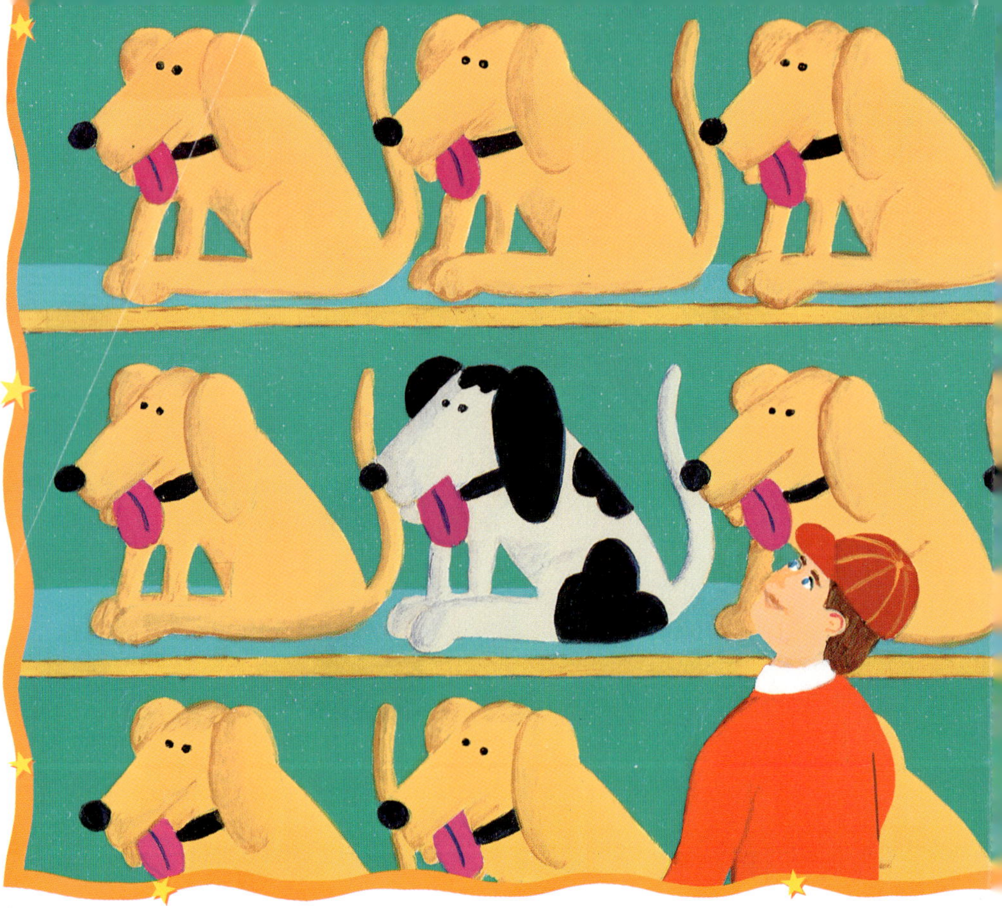

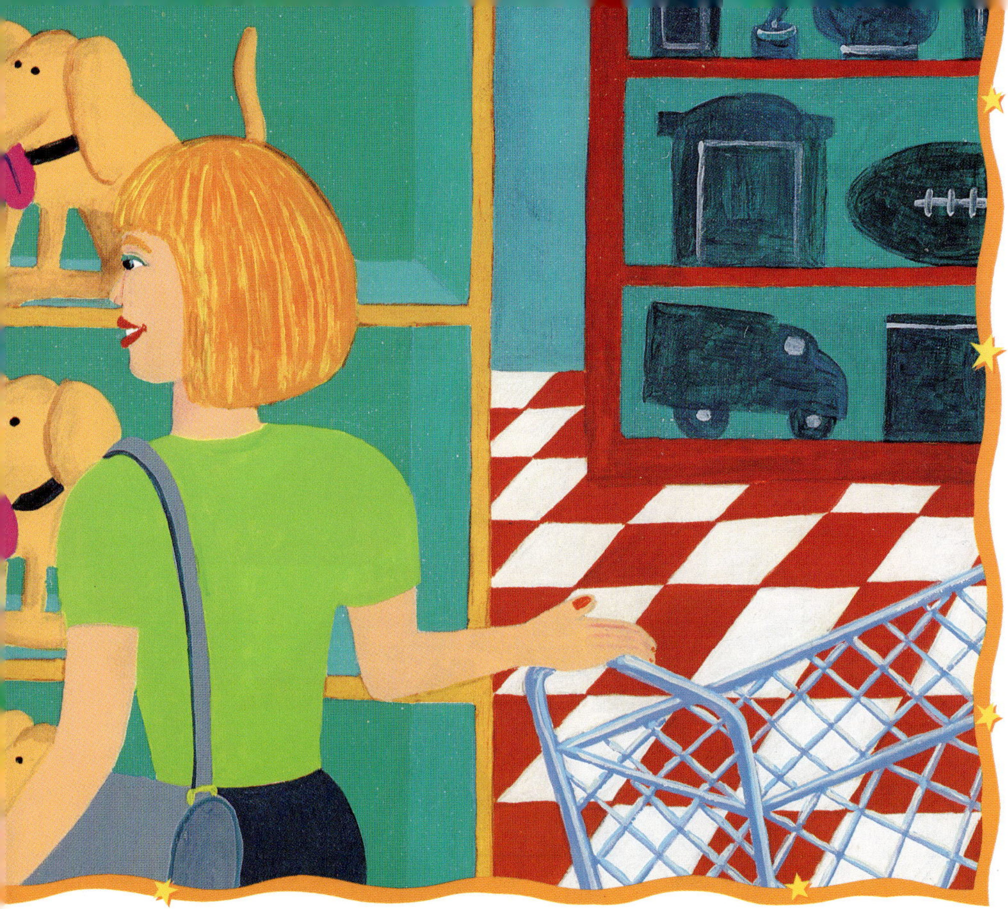

the dog

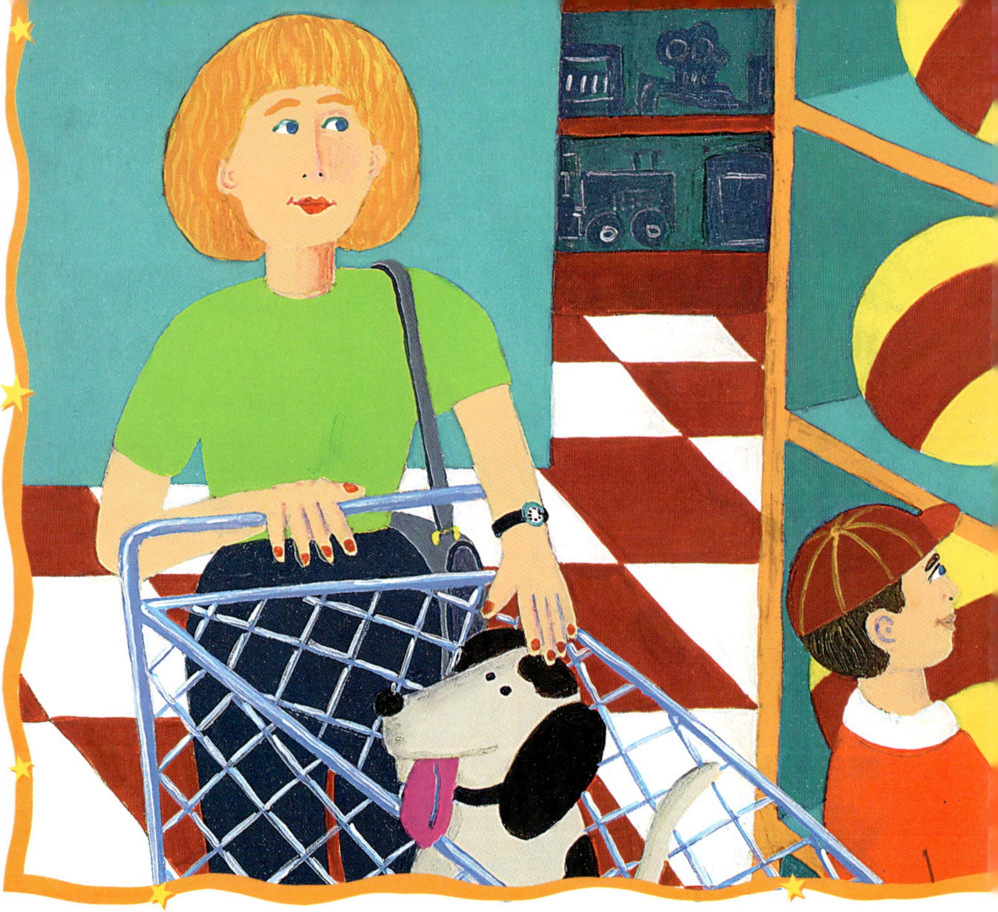

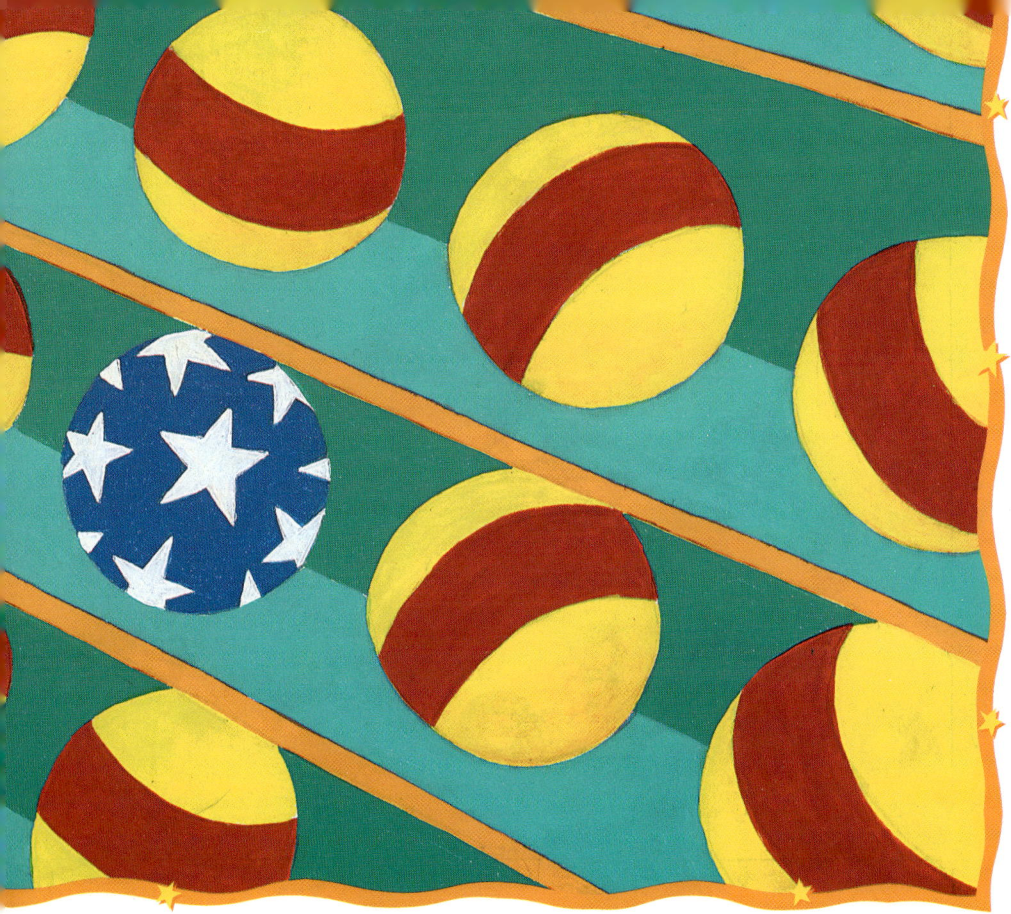

the ball

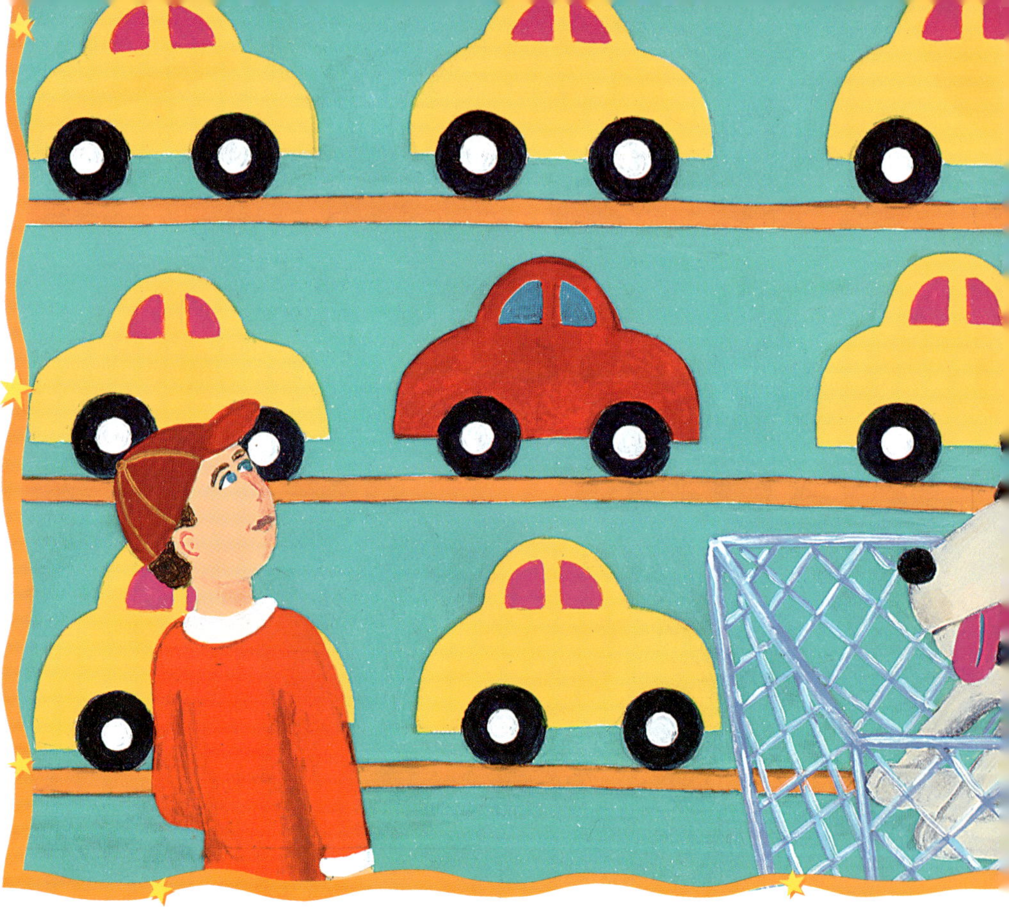

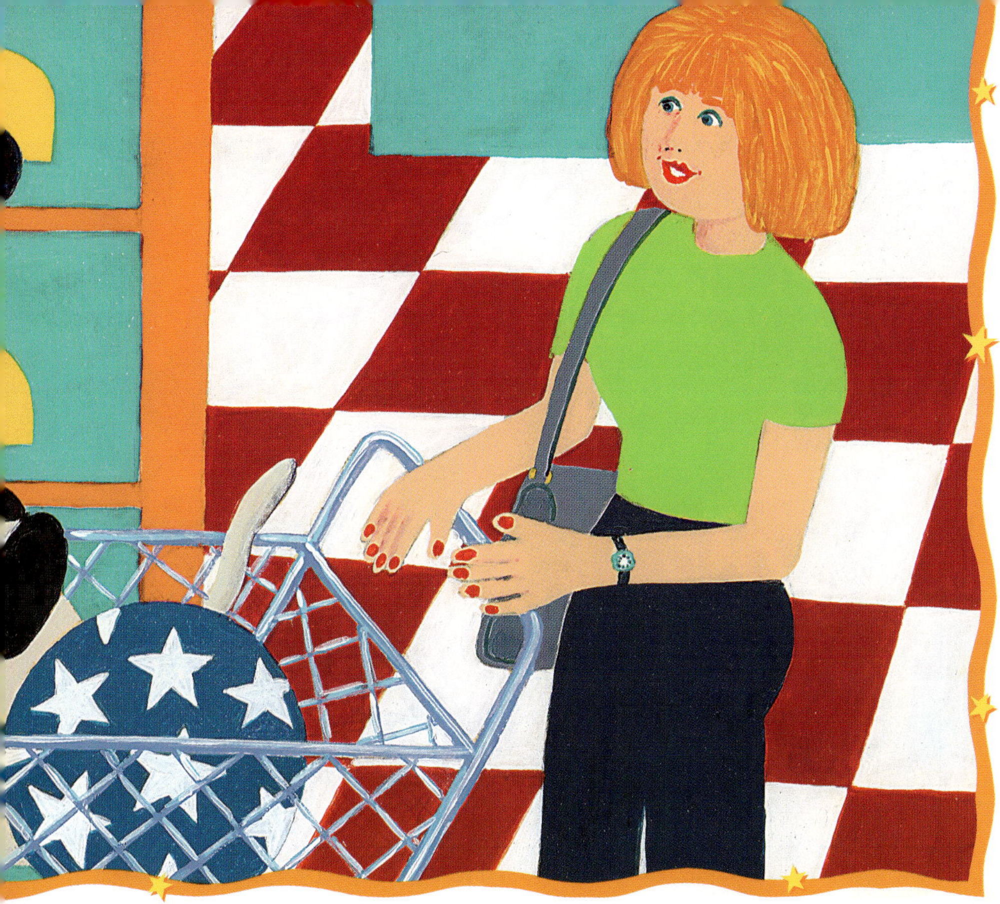

the car

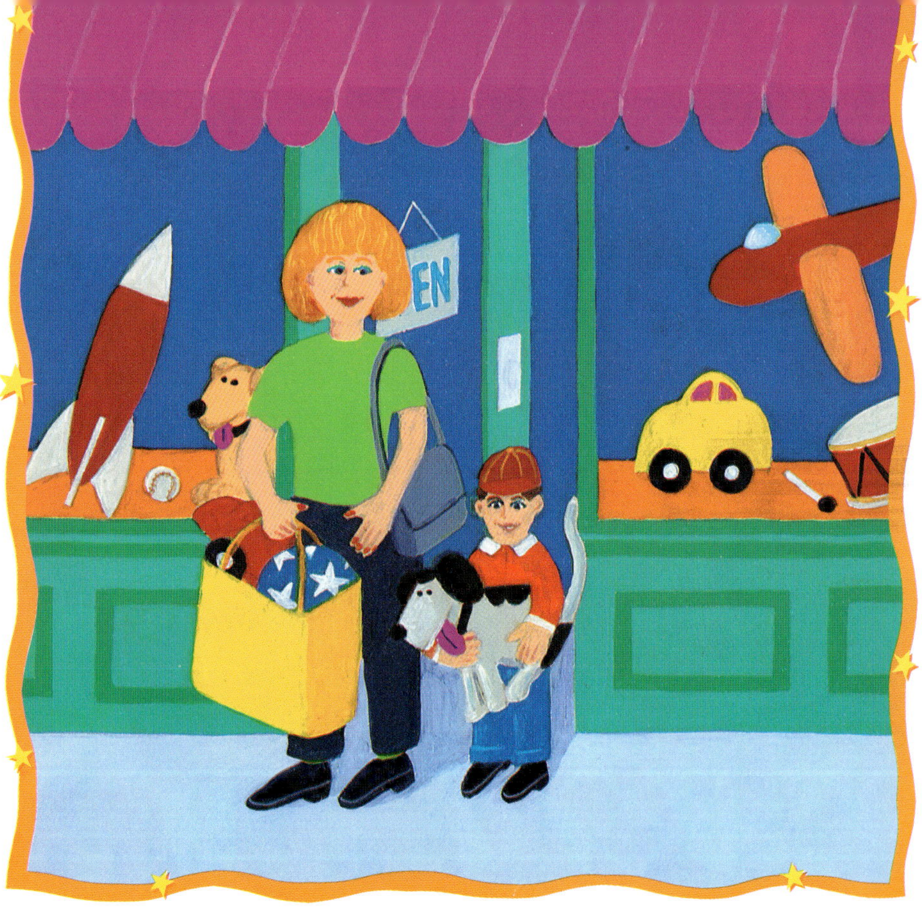

the toys